CROSS CULTURAL COMMUNICATION

A Visual Approach

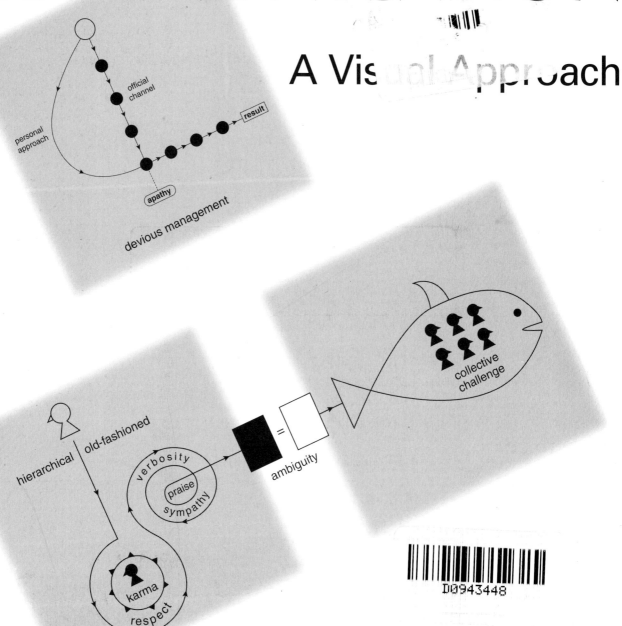

Transcreen Publications

Cross Cultural Communication - A Visual Approach

First published in 1999 by
Transcreen Publications
Riversdown, Warnford
Hampshire, SO32 3LH
United Kingdom

Tel. +44 1962 771111
Fax +44 1962 771104
Email richard.lewis@crossculture.com

ISBN 0 9534398 0 2

Printed in Great Britain by
Axis Europe Limited, London.

CROSS CULTURAL COMMUNICATION

A Visual Approach

Richard D. Lewis

Transscreen Publications

Contents

Audience expectations

Leadership styles

Language of management

Introduction

Communication – verbal communication, that is – appears on the surface to be a relatively simple operation requiring two basic components – a speaker and a listener.

But we know it is a more complex process than that. Even when two people with a similar cultural background are involved, there are several stages between delivery and comprehension. First, **words** are spoken, but the actual **message** emerges only when the words are considered **in context**. What is said must be evaluated against the background of how it was said, when and where, who said it and why. There is also the **filter** created by the speaker's personality and psychological make-up.

The listening process, too, is complicated. Firstly the listener had certain **expectations** which were or were not met. The **filter** of the listener's personality colours the speech he/she hears. An **interpretation** is placed on the words, thus defining the **message** for the recipient. The intended message and the received one are rarely the same.

When the speaker and listener are from different cultures, the odds against an accurate interpretation of the message are great. Diverse backgrounds of history, customs, traditions and taboos, as well as the accepted manners of communicating in different parts of the world, interfere with straight comprehension. Speech is often intended to **influence** or **manipulate** our fellow man. **Leadership** and some form of **dominance** are often involved. Finally each language of the world has certain **in-built characteristics**, often unperceived by the people who speak them.

In each culture the patterns of communication, listening and manipulation are remarkably consistent. Once these are recognized by an outsider, the behaviour of the cultural group becomes more predictable. This booklet purports to give the international traveller a quick reference guide, in diagrammatic form, as to how different nationals expect to communicate with and influence interlocutors, audiences, colleagues and business partners.

Communication patterns
at meetings

Meetings give individuals a chance to communicate – to use their speech skills to good effect. Speech is certainly a personal weapon, but different cultures use it in diverse ways.

Perhaps the most basic use of speech is to give and receive information. Germans, Finns, Dutch people are good at conveying facts, figures, etc. quickly and efficiently. Other cultures believe speech can be a much more powerful weapon in terms of eloquence, fluency and persuasion. Italians, particularly, believe they can convince anyone of just about anything, provided they gain sufficient personal access. French, Spaniards, South Americans use speech to great effect and at length, though Nordics and some Anglo-Saxons find it all too much at times.

Indians are very fond of flowery Victorian-like speech to inspire people – Russians like to search their souls verbally, Confucian and South-East Asian cultures use speech as a give-and-receive-respect mechanism and establish relative status and rank in a few sentences. Americans often launch into speech with business or selling in mind. Arabs use it in a didactic or moralistic manner.

In some less democratic societies, speech may be used for coercion, propaganda or deception. In some cultures, speech can be deployed in such a vague way that it actually clouds issues rather than clarifies them. English and Japanese people can waffle and stall with ease, while Chinese and Polynesians excel in ambiguity.

Silence itself is a form of speech when applied at appropriate moments and should not be interrupted! Finns and Japanese are past-masters at soothing or strategic silences.

Australians regard suitably broad speech as a mechanism for a manager to show solidarity with "the mates".

Finally some nationalities seem to love speech for the sake of speech itself, taking the stage to hear their own voice. French, Spanish and Greek people often perorate in this manner. They are not popular with Nordics and most Asians.

Australia

Australian meetings are in the main relatively informal affairs, beginning with cups of tea and first names and ending in compromise where everyone feels he/she has taken away something. In between, exchanges can be lively, blunt, cynical, even aggressive, though in general the participants are looking for solutions. With foreigners, Australians make efforts to curb their national irreverence for superiors and institutions.

Germany

Germans are much more concerned with protocol and conduct orderly meetings which are supposed to end successfully, as one discovers "the truth" – that is to say, that the discussions are based on real facts and sound information. This agenda-bound, laborious style often seems heavy to some nationalities, but at least one knows where one stands and where one is heading.

Australia

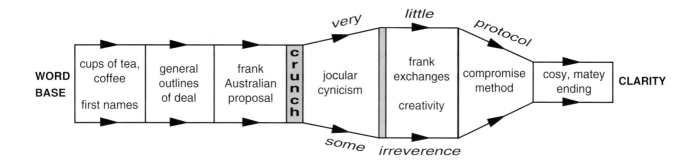

Germany

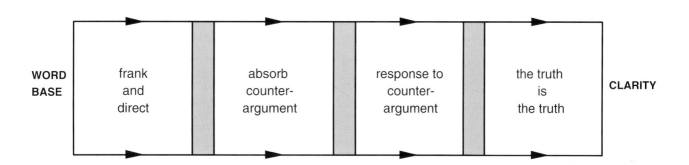

USA

In the USA one puts one's cards on the table at the beginning and spells it all out again in louder English for foreigners who hesitate. When Americans feel they are getting bogged down, they use sarcasm and provocative measures to get the meeting going. For them a real fight is communication. Amongst themselves, they push the other side to the limit and then make quick, mutual concessions to make sure the deal goes through. Formal negotiators such as French, Germans and Japanese find this style somewhat disconcerting.

UK

In the UK a meeting will probably be concluded successfully if one doesn't "rock the boat". Humour, understatement, vagueness, stalling, re-packaging and a sprinkling of white lies are all weapons for keeping it all jolly nice, chaps.

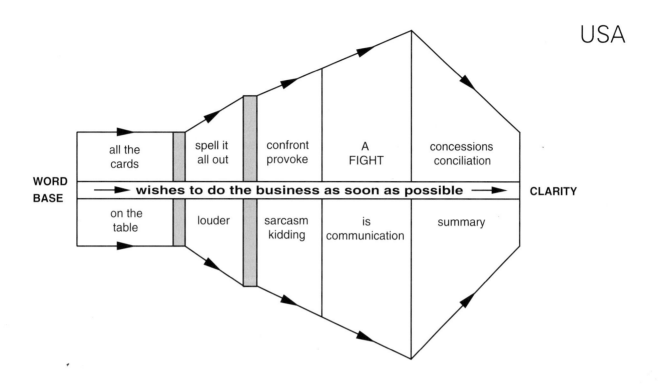

USA

all the cards		spell it all out		confront provoke	A FIGHT	concessions conciliation

WORD BASE → **wishes to do the business as soon as possible** → **CLARITY**

on the table		louder		sarcasm kidding	is communication	summary

UK

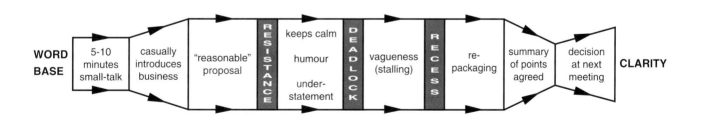

WORD BASE | 5-10 minutes small-talk | casually introduces business | "reasonable" proposal | RESISTANCE | keeps calm humour under-statement | DEADLOCK | vagueness (stalling) | RECESS | re-packaging | summary of points agreed | decision at next meeting | **CLARITY**

" don't rock the boat "

Japan

In Japan what is actually said at a meeting has little or no importance. The manner of address, showing the correct amount of respect, progresses the business. Japanese do not seriously negotiate during meetings, but in informal sessions outside. They have no authority to change the company position on the spot.

France

The French are well-trained orators who try to crush their opponents with icy, Cartesian logic. This style, enhanced by their fecund imagination, makes them very difficult to beat in theoretical discussion. The only way to stop them perorating is to agree with them early on.

Japan

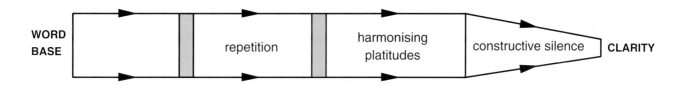

France

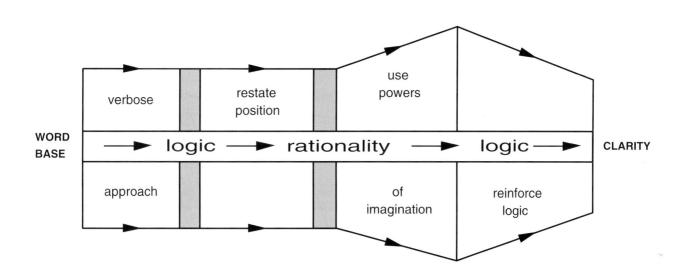

Sweden

Swedes are fond of attending meetings which they set up with the proper protocol. Amongst themselves they go on endlessly, but, when running up against foreign resistance, they ask for adjournment, so they can form a proper Swedish consensus. This tactic leads to considerable delays and frustrates go-getters like Americans, who wish to see early action. Swedish fondness for doing things the Swedish way often poses problems.

Spain

Spanish proposals at meetings are usually delivered in theatrical, declamatory fashion, which means that if they are delivered by a VIP, they are virtually irreversible. In such situations it is better to agree with everything, as Spanish luminaries cannot stand being opposed in public. Speakers begin to like and develop a loyalty towards compliant foreigners, to whom they are well disposed to make concessions over dinner later.

Sweden

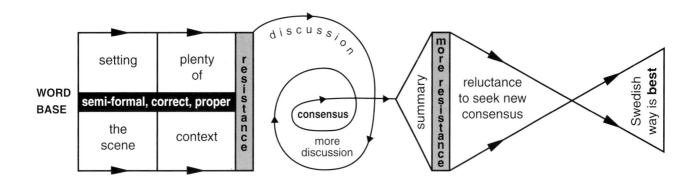

Spain

Norway

Meetings in Norway are frank, healthy occasions where one gets quickly to the point and gets one's feelings off one's chest in a good-humoured fashion. Deviousness is taboo and once one has obtained a clear view of the big picture, agreement is usually achieved. Once a decision has been reached, it is not likely to be changed.

Denmark

Danes believe they can carry everybody (especially foreigners) by charm (in Danish *hygge*) and seem to agree to all proposals well into the negotiation. They are skilful at subtle re-packaging and therefore have to be watched carefully. They are not happy at being "roped in", but maintain equanimity with an eye to future business.

Norway

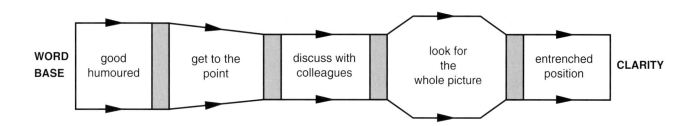

Denmark

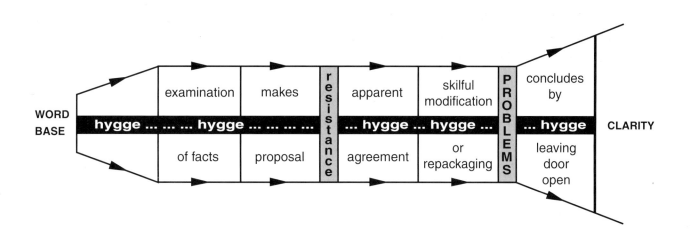

Finland

At meetings, Finns believe in saying only that which is absolutely necessary. Like the Japanese, they do not really trust words. If their original proposal is considered unclear, they repeat it in summarised form, assuming that is the best route to clarity. ("What I really meant was A, B and C"). An Italian counterpart sits waiting for the rest of the alphabet!

Italy

Italians deliver their proposals at length (probably with ten times as many words as the Finns). If they are then required to clarify or disagreed with, they do the opposite of the Finns – they become more explicit and may launch into a half hour clarification of the original proposal. In Italy, words cost nothing.

Finland

WORD
BASE   minimal speech   increase succinctness   CLARITY

Italy

WORD
BASE   verbose   miscomprehension   increase in   flexibility   CLARITY
              approach   verbosity

Hispanic America

Meetings with Hispanic Americans are more complicated than with say Nordics or Australians. To begin with a lot of small talk is expected and Americans and Northern Europeans would have to give clear signs of respecting the national honour of their counterparts. Initial proposals are often far removed from realistic conclusions and protracted haggling is part of the process. Agreements reached are often somewhat inconclusive and strict adherence to contract is questionable.

Brazil

In Brazil, meetings are equally verbose and human feelings take precedence over close examination of the facts. Brazilians are rarely the bearers of bad news and a certain amount of healthy scepticism is advisable. Leisurely haggling often leads to satisfactory agreements, though it is as well to summarize carefully what all parties are supposed to do.

Hispanic America

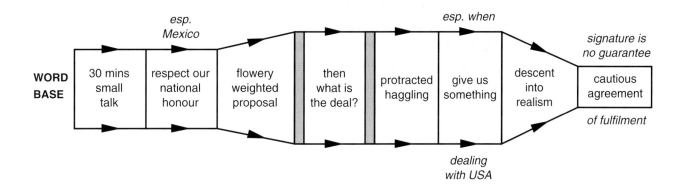

Brazil

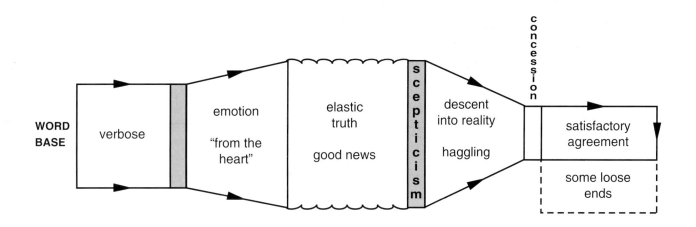

Netherlands

The pragmatic Dutch, though mainly concerned with facts and figures, are also great talkers and rarely make final decisions without a long "Dutch" debate, sometimes running the danger of over-analysis. Foreign counterparts are also subjected to this and routinely tested for bluffing, as Dutch people with their long international experience in business, hate to think of themselves as being in any way gullible.

Indonesia

Indonesians excel in respect language and, in the reactive manner, modify their own proposals out of deference. They are clever at saying what you want to hear. They can engage in prolonged, childlike questioning to clarify intent, though meetings often end with a few loose ends floating around. They can be tantalisingly ambiguous.

Netherlands

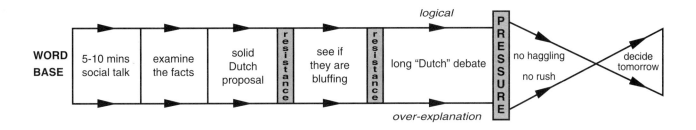

Indonesia

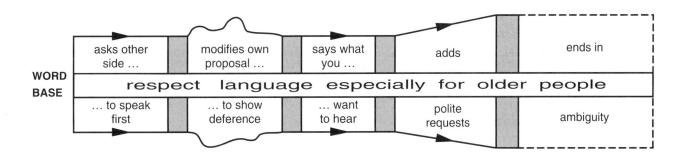

China

Chinese attend meetings in sizeable numbers and negotiate collectively. The problem for Westerners is that there is generally some state involvement and the real decision-makers are not actually in the meetings. Patient and courteous discussion is normal, but a frequent tactic is "tough talk" in fits and starts. Everyone protects everyone's face, though the Chinese often moralise about Western decadence.

Korea

Koreans believe they can handle Westerners better than other Orientals can and often try their hand at humour. They have a very elastic concept of truth and it is advisable to double check anything that is promised. They often are looking for quick profits and one should be careful about granting exclusivity. It is better to judge their statements against past performance rather than future forecasts.

China

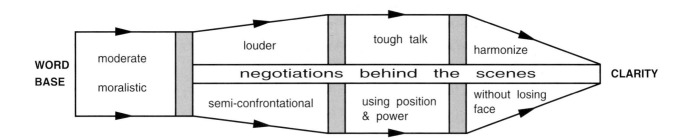

Korea

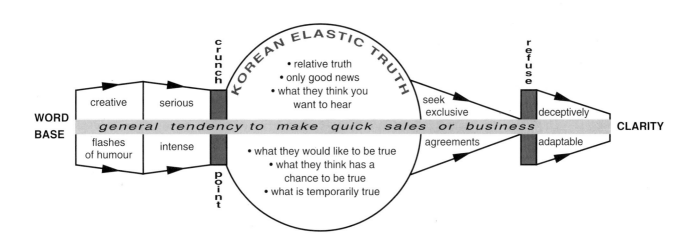

Canada

Canadians are among the most reasonable people in the world to negotiate with and meetings are normally conducted in a pleasant, open manner aiming at a win-win result. They move quickly towards implementation and their lean style suits both action-oriented Americans and low key Brits, Nordics and Asians. Canadians make good chairmen in international meetings.

Russia

The atmosphere at Russian meetings depends very much on the context. In Soviet times one was engaged in long-drawn out, cautious discussions with frequently intransigent civil servants. Russians of all categories know how to blow hot and cold and can be theatrically verbose as well as icily tight-lipped. In the current fluid situation Russian entrepreneurs are opportunistic and of many ethnic backgrounds (Armenians and Georgians are ubiquitous) and while they are more flexible than state officials, they are unlikely to be very accommodating and conduct negotiations in "chess tempo".

Canada

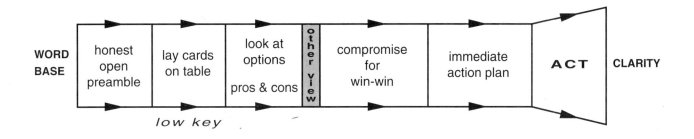

Russia

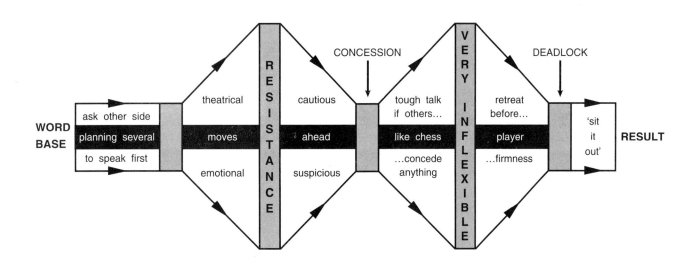

India

A meeting in India can be a kind of aesthetic experience where flowery, Victorian English can set the scene for exaggerated deference and flattering approaches. Indians, like Danes, maintain the semi-euphoric atmosphere as long as possible, before some holes are detected in the apparently agreed arrangement. Indians remain polite while modifications are proposed and re-package energetically to reach an agreement. They hate turning any business down.

Arab countries

One-to-one meetings are hard to come by in the Arab world, where a retinue or number of individuals share the "open office" of a VIP. Senior Arabs, though benign, often adopt a moralistic tone to younger Westerners, also to other Arabs. When their proposals are opposed, they become rhetorical and eyes can flash with passion or anger. In general they are amenable, particularly if they perceive the other side as being sincere.

India

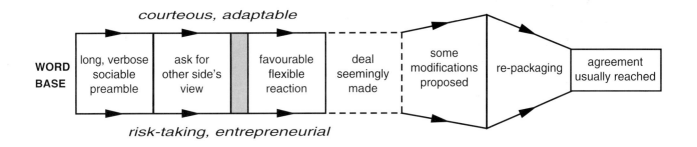

courteous, adaptable

WORD BASE → long, verbose sociable preamble → ask for other side's view → favourable flexible reaction → deal seemingly made → some modifications proposed → re-packaging → agreement usually reached

risk-taking, entrepreneurial

Arab countries

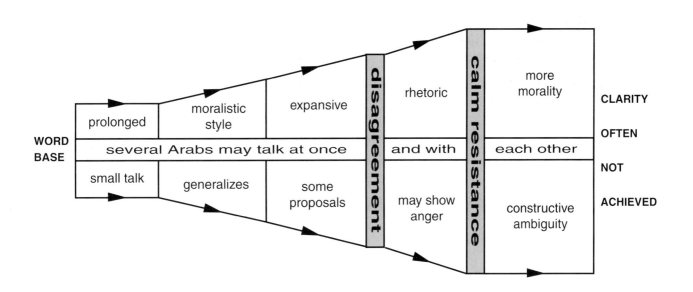

WORD BASE → prolonged → moralistic style → expansive → disagreement → rhetoric → calm resistance → more morality → **CLARITY**

several Arabs may talk at once / and with / each other — **OFTEN**

small talk → generalizes → some proposals → may show anger → constructive ambiguity — **NOT ACHIEVED**

Listening habits

Captive audiences generally appear to listen, but in fact they listen to different degrees and in different ways. There are good listeners and bad listeners. Others, such as the Americans, listen carefully or indifferently, depending on the nature of the address.

Although each nationality has its own specific style of listening, one can divide them into rough categories, where certain generalisations apply. For instance Nordics (Danes, Finns, Norwegians and Swedes) could readily be described as the best listeners, partly because their own natural reticence gives them no incentive to interrupt. Calm concentration is a strong point.

Germanic peoples are also good listeners. Both Germans and Dutch are hungry for the facts, though the latter wish to start a debate fairly soon. Disciplined Germans have perhaps the longest attention span of any nationality, diligently making notes as they listen.

As far as the Anglo-Saxons are concerned, English and Canadians pay polite attention as long as the speaker is reasonably low key. Debate is required afterwards. Australians are more cynical and can't take too much seriousness, but, like Americans, will listen well if technical information is being imparted. Americans, used to show business and encapsulated news items, tend to lose concentration if they are not entertained in some way.

In ex-Communist countries e.g. Russia, Poland and the Baltic states, listening habits are directly and strongly affected by previous and recent political control (propaganda). Most Eastern Europeans believe all official statements are lies and that any changes introduced by the authorities are for the worse. Speakers must therefore combat automatic scepticism in these cultures. This is compounded in Russia by an inherent suspicion of foreigners. Hungarians tend to be less apathetic than some of the others.

Countries which have had a colonial past – India, Malaysia, Indonesia – also listen with a certain amount of suspicion, though they can be won over by an eloquent and thoroughly respectful speaker. Reaction is, however, deceptive, since listeners in these areas give feedback which they think will please. They also are reluctant to admit to gaps in comprehension.

As we go further east, the Confucian cultures of China, Japan and Korea have language problems and are also reluctant to confess to non-comprehension. What they listen for principally is exaggerated respect from the speaker, so that nobody loses face. Chinese and Koreans are traditionally suspicious of Westerners. The Japanese are more open to address, but so involved with politeness and vague expressions that messages often do not get across.

Latins are not very attentive listeners in principle, as they are normally anxious to speak themselves. A charismatic speaker may hold them for 30 minutes or more, but the French in particular do not believe that foreigners can teach them very much. Italians have busy minds and wander. Spaniards dislike monologues – they want to interject and argue vigorously. Latin Americans show interest in new ideas, but are somewhat sceptical about European caution and even more so about US exploitation.

Arabs are not good listeners when they are in groups, though they like an extra talk afterwards in private. They are defensive about Islam.

Africans listen respectfully in order to learn and acquire know-how, though they need to have things spelled out slowly and tend to be fatalistic about outcomes.

All in all, it is advisable for speakers, salesmen, presenters etc. to familiarize themselves as much as possible in advance with the traditional expectations of the audience to be addressed. Style and content should be adapted accordingly.

Germany

Germans, hungry for information and technical details, are among the world's best listeners. Price-conscious and needing lots of context, they become suspicious if things sound too simple.

USA

Americans are also keen on acquiring technical details, but, used to show business, their attention wanders if speakers are boring. They expect and appreciate a hard sell.

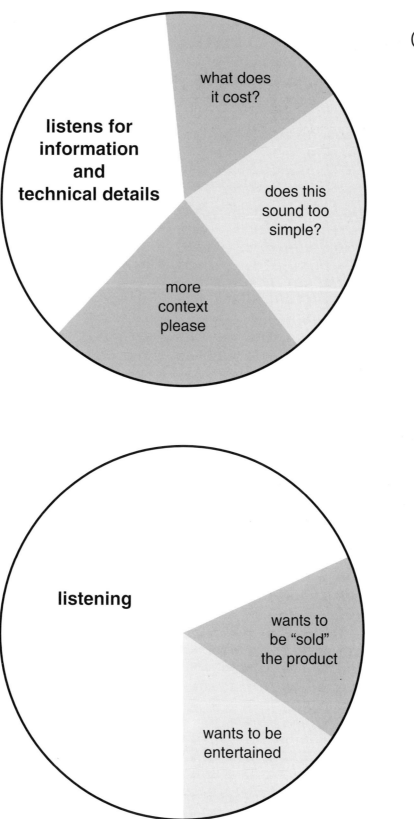

Germany

USA

Finland

Nobody listens more carefully than the Finns who, according to tradition, never interrupt a speaker. The price of their attention is one cup of coffee per hour. They give no feedback.

Sweden

Cooperative listeners who give encouraging, whispered feedback during the presentation. They want facts and technical details and an enormous amount of context. As consensus is obligatory in Sweden, they are nervous about what others in the audience may be thinking.

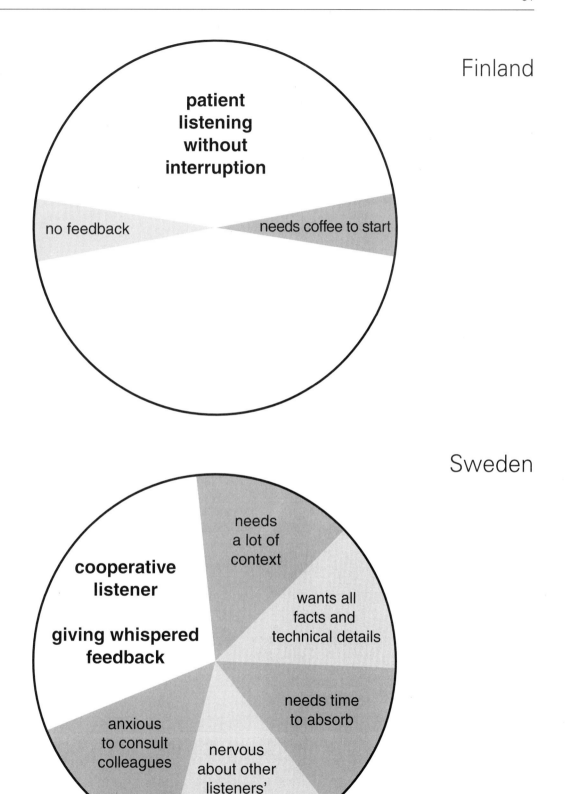

Finland

patient
listening
without
interruption

no feedback

needs coffee to start

Sweden

cooperative
listener

giving whispered
feedback

needs
a lot of
context

wants all
facts and
technical details

needs time
to absorb

nervous
about other
listeners'
opinions

anxious
to consult
colleagues

Denmark

Danes make a pleasant smiling audience, but in fact hide a healthy dose of cynicism. They create counter-proposals while listening and give immediate feedback. Speakers should be modest and humorous.

Norway

Norwegians listen in good humour, but quickly develop strong opinions which they soon expose. They are data-oriented, but appreciate a personal touch. Norway-centred.

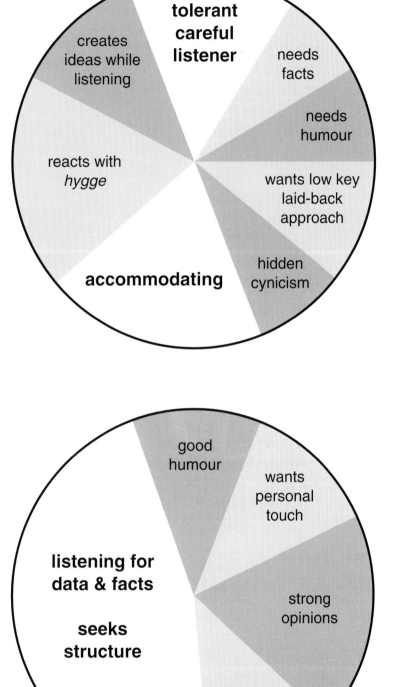

Denmark

- tolerant careful listener
- needs facts
- needs humour
- wants low key laid-back approach
- hidden cynicism
- accommodating
- reacts with *hygge*
- creates ideas while listening

Norway

- good humour
- wants personal touch
- strong opinions
- Norway is best
- listening for data & facts
- seeks structure

France

French are among the worst listeners in the world. A firm belief in their own intellectual superiority makes them reluctant to be guided by people from other cultures. The attitude is: we probably know already, French is best anyhow, we have busy minds, so say something interesting and make it quick.

Japan

Japanese audiences are disciplined and attentive, but understand virtually nothing in any foreign language spoken at normal speed. They do not come to understand, they are there to be courteous and create personal harmony. How you address them is what matters. What you say is irrelevant. (They will get the information they need from your printed material).

France

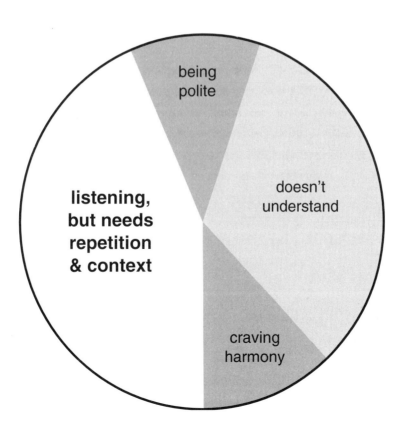

Japan

Spain

Spaniards are not dedicated listeners. They read less than any other people in Europe and pay little attention to the content of presentations. They do, however, watch you carefully and sum you up by observing your physical characteristics, your mannerisms and your willingness to participate in the congenial and jocular socialising which will inevitably follow. You need to be imaginative to hold their attention for more than 20 minutes.

Italy

Italians appear to pay more attention than Spaniards during presentations, but in fact it is a toss-up. Their busy minds are formulating their reply, which they will deliver as soon as you pause long enough for them to get in. They are anxious to engage you in a dialogue which will soon define the relationship between you.

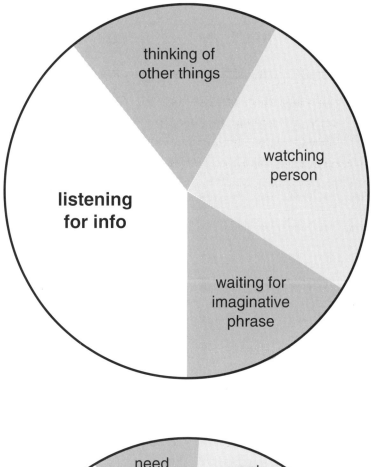

Spain

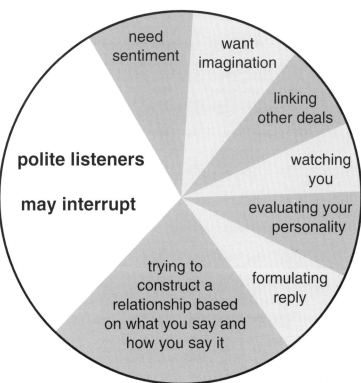

Italy

Australia

It is fatal to talk posh or be in any way pompous in front of Australians, who have a healthy and enduring disrespect for anyone in a superior position or who seeks to promote oneself. It is also inadvisable to be too serious or complicated. Australians are fond of jokes and anecdotes, preferably delivered in broad speech. A friendly and lively audience once they have decided to like you.

Canada

Canadians like modest, unpretentious speakers who provide facts without trimmings and inject gentle humour in the process. Unlike Americans, they do not want the hard sell. They enjoy early debate with you, but listen politely to all you have to say first.

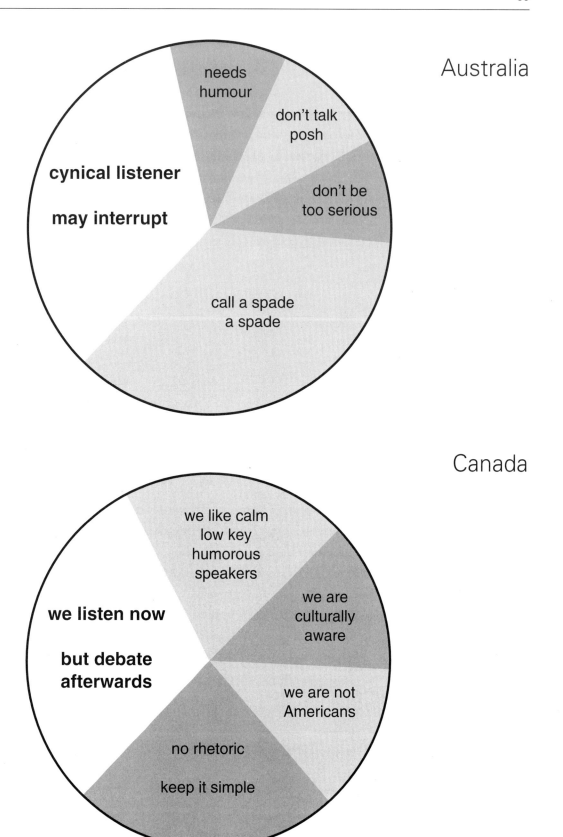

Hispanic America

Most Hispanic Americans are loquacious Latins who have been exploited sometime in the past by Americans or Europeans. Traditionally they are poor at cooperating with authorities or any external plans which do not correspond to their immediate needs. Consequently they are not among the best of audiences. Only charismatic speakers can get them to listen long, and even they must be very respectful and present the listeners with an intrinsic learning opportunity.

Brazil

Among South Americans, Brazilians are perhaps the most receptive to foreign ideas, perhaps because their break with their colonial masters – Portugal – was amicable. The key to their attention is to talk enough about Brazil (even Brazilian football) and be invariably cheerful bordering on euphoric. They are not really recording efficiently what you actually say, but eagerly seeking *simpatísmo* to enable them to do business with someone they like.

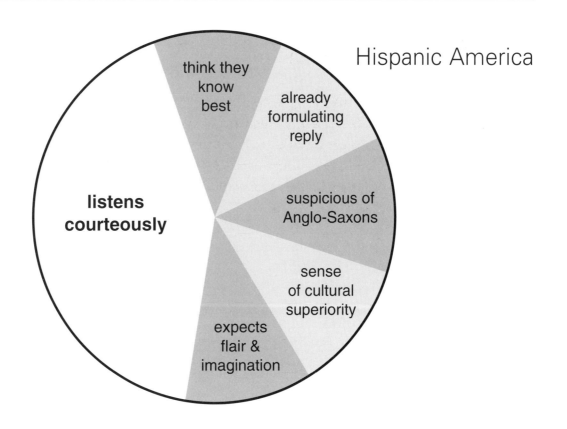

Hispanic America

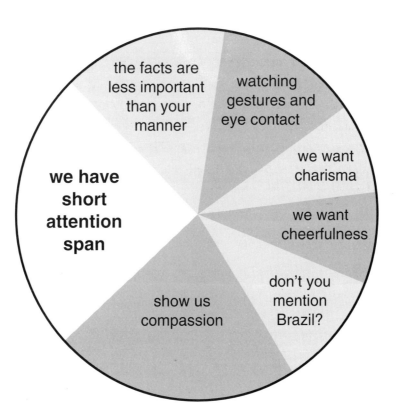

Brazil

China

Mainland Chinese are eager to acquire know-how from Westerners and Western markets for their products. They listen carefully and patiently in these areas, though most audiences are heavily dependent on interpreters. The manner of the speaker is considered more important than the content, so one needs to inject sufficient flattery and protect everyone's face. They are traditionally suspicious of "foreign devils", so work hard at creating trust.

Korea

Protection of face *(kibun)* is also of paramount importance among Koreans, who traditionally dislike foreigners, but disguise it well. Audiences are respectful, but Koreans like to show that they handle Westerners well and they often give lively feedback and ask original questions. They even like Western humour (which they profess to understand) so the odd joke or two might be attempted to soften them up.

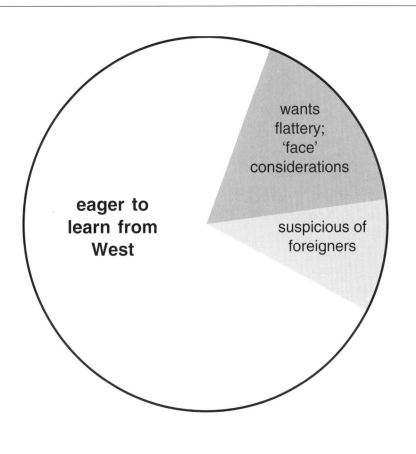

China

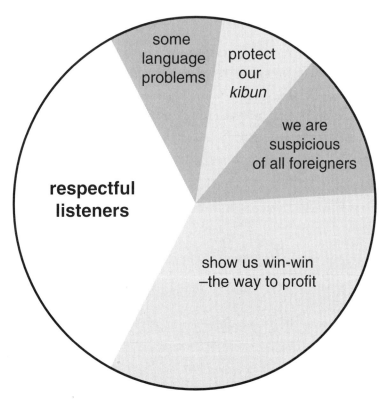

Korea

UK

British people, with their debating traditions, must listen well in order to construct their reply. Polite listening is mandatory, though one may occasionally interrupt. British speakers would normally be rather understated and include humour, so foreign speakers would do well to follow suit. Feedback is often lively and productive.

Netherlands

Dutch audiences are both easy and difficult: easy in the sense that they are hungry for information and good ideas, difficult because they are very experienced and not open to much persuasion by others. Like the French, they tend to "know it all", but will in fact accept and seize viable plans and projects which are presented vigorously and backed-up with convincing evidence.

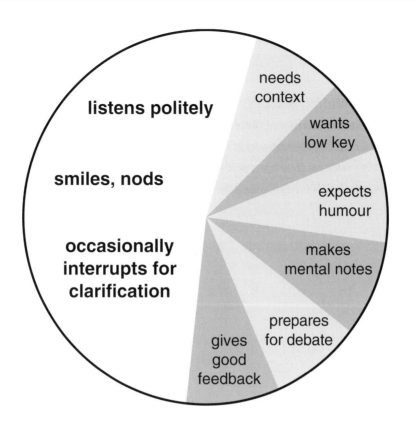

UK

- **listens politely**
- **smiles, nods**
- **occasionally interrupts for clarification**
- needs context
- wants low key
- expects humour
- makes mental notes
- prepares for debate
- gives good feedback

Netherlands

- **we listen but prefer dialogue**
- ideas are objective and independent of the people uttering them
- cautious sceptical listeners
- no hard sell
- not too much persuasion
- we are very experienced
- hard facts please

Arab countries

Arabs listen better individually than in groups. A less than charismatic speaker may find they talk while he does. They listen defensively where Islam and some political problems are concerned. Speakers should maintain strong eye contact, get close to them, flatter a bit and raise the voice to indicate sincerity. After a general presentation, many Arabs come to the speaker for extra, private information.

India

The key to Indian attention is to be eloquent, humble and respectful. They like flowery speech and an extensive vocabulary. They are willing to listen at length, to enable a relationship to develop and their aim, in the subsequent feedback, is to make a friend of the speaker. Not difficult audiences, but their sagacity must not be underestimated.

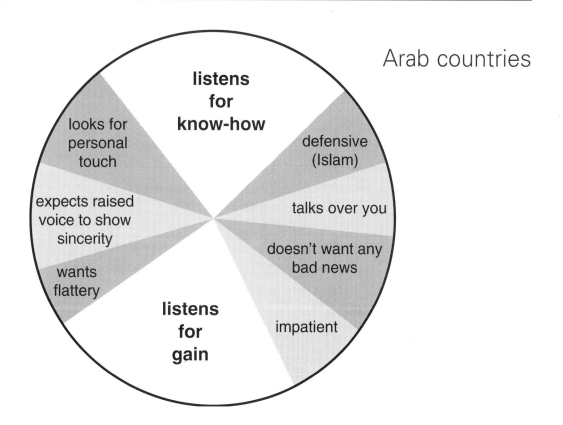

Arab countries

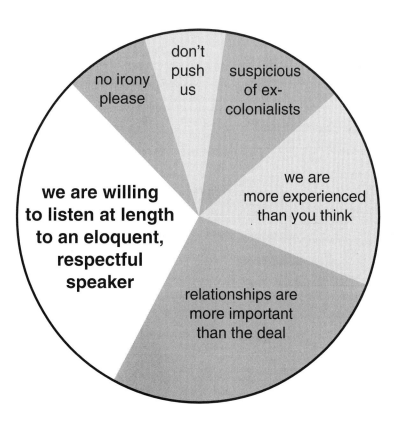

India

Indonesia

Indonesians, like Malaysians and other S.E. Asian people, are respectful listeners. Unlike Malaysians, they are often deficient in language skills and need careful repetition of all key points. Their questioning can be very simple, almost childlike; they rarely say anything to offend. Consequently it is often difficult to judge the relative success of one's presentation.

Africa

Africans like slow, clear presentations and are suspicious of hurried communication. The approach must be simple, warm and personal – trust-building. Fatalism may lead to apathy, and enthusiasm and persuasion are needed to combat this.

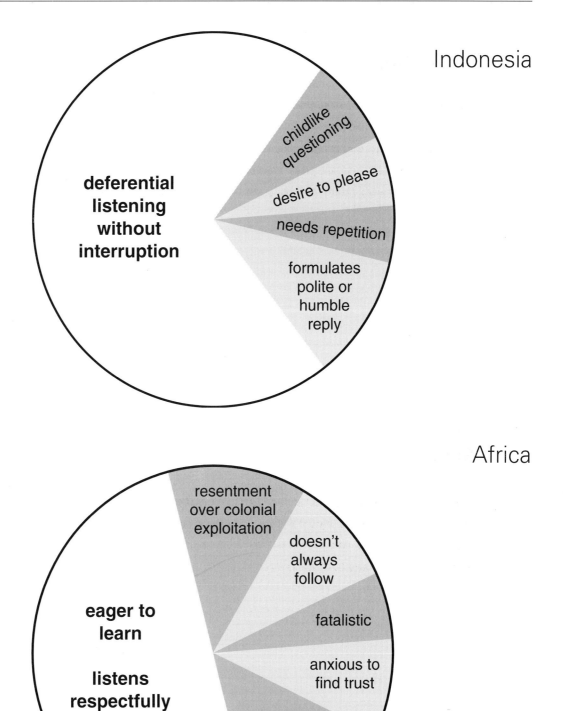

Russia

Russians automatically distrust official statements, whether made by governments, state agencies or big multinationals. Personal messages, even rumour, ring true. Russians listen best, in small numbers or privately, to a person who presents an opportunity, shares their fate and conspires to "beat the system". Speakers, especially foreigners, should be blunt, confiding and obviate any deviousness.

Hungary

Hungarians, who are dying to speak themselves, are not the best of listeners and behave impolitely in the presence of a boring speaker. As they consider themselves sophisticated, ingredients necessary for holding their attention are charisma, humour, a challenge and brevity. They are interested in change, but are cautious if it is proposed by official sources.

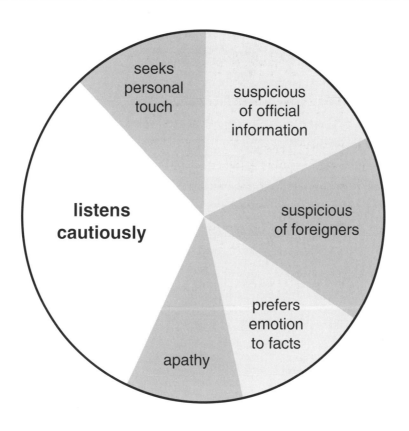

Russia

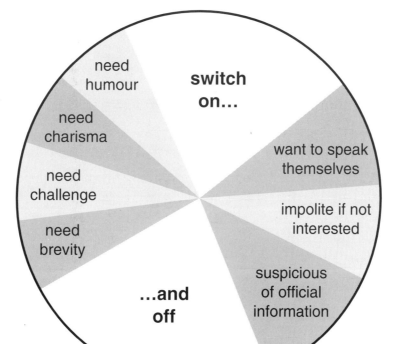

Hungary

Poland and the Baltic States

Poland and the three Baltic states have been fed on political and economic propaganda for decades and simply distrust any statement which emanates from official or semi-official sources. The key to their attention is to address very personal messages and proposals to future business partners. Estonians are the easiest, being especially receptive to next-of-kin Finns. Latvians are dutiful listeners who provide little feedback. Lithuanians, persuasive people themselves, listen more impatiently. Poles are not only sceptical, but easily insulted, so one must be careful with words. All these countries now face west, however, so that there is a basic desire to be persuaded, once trust is established.

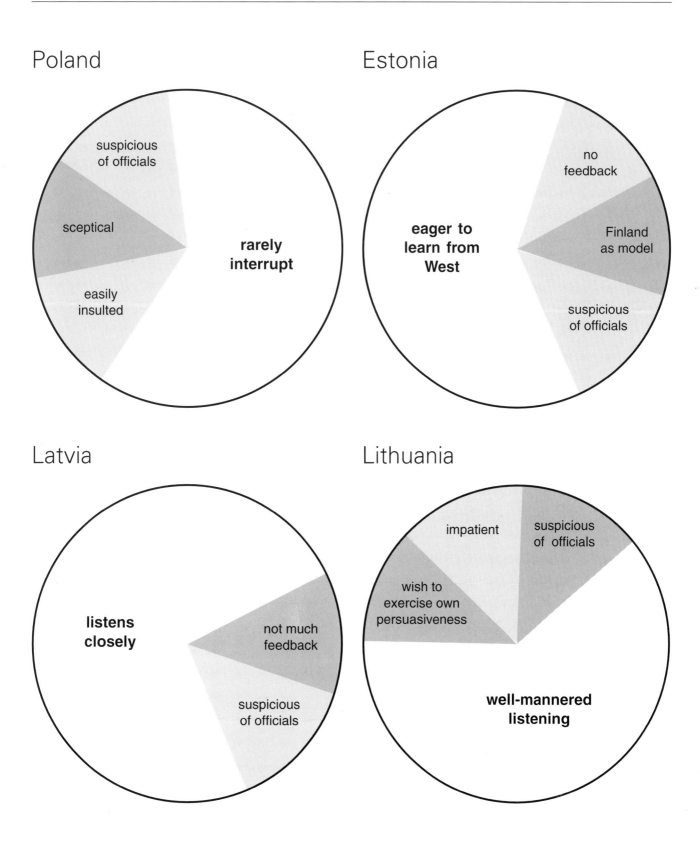

Poland

- suspicious of officials
- sceptical
- easily insulted
- **rarely interrupt**

Estonia

- no feedback
- Finland as model
- suspicious of officials
- **eager to learn from West**

Latvia

- **listens closely**
- not much feedback
- suspicious of officials

Lithuania

- impatient
- suspicious of officials
- wish to exercise own persuasiveness
- **well-mannered listening**

Audience expectations
during presentations

U.S.A.
• humour
• joking
• modernity
• gimmicks
• slogans
• catch phrases
• hard sell

U.K.
• humour
• a story
• "nice" product
• reasonable price
• quality
• traditional rather than modern

Germany
• solidity of company
• solidity of product
• technical info
• context
• beginning – middle – ending
• lots of print
• no jokes
• good price
• quality
• delivery date

France
• formality
• innovative product
• "sexy" appeal
• imagination
• logical presentation
• reference to France
• style, appearance
• personal touch
• may interrupt

Japan
• good price
• USP
• synergy with Co. image
• harmony
• politeness
• respect for their Co.
• good name of your Co.
• quiet presentation
• well-dressed presenter
• formality
• diagrams

Sweden
• modernity
• quality
• design
• technical info
• delivery dates

Arab countries

- rhetoric
- eloquence
- liveliness
- personal touch
- clean appearance
- education
- know-how
- respect
- physical proximity
- strong eye contact
- wants "extra talk" afterwards

Finland

- modernity
- quality
- technical info
- modest presentation
- design

Australia

- matey opening
- informality throughout
- humour
- persuasive style
- no padding
- little contexting
- innovative product
- essential technical info
- personal touch
- may interrupt
- imaginative conclusion

China

- know-how
- humble tone
- reserve and patience
- investment from you
- long term view
- licensing
- help and advice
- equality of treatment
- older speakers
- respect for their elders

Korea

- respect
- reserve
- hard facts
- clear English
- well-dressed
- need trust
- win-win prospect
- the way to profit
- quick solutions
- some humour

Denmark

- best design
- quality
- delivery date
- modernity
- quiet, rational presentation
- humour
- technical
- no bombast

Indonesia

- courtesy & gentleness
- friendliness
- relations more important than profits
- quiet presentation
- neat appearance
- no hurry
- focus on Indonesia's achievements rather than shortcomings
- everything is negotiable

India

- humility
- flowery speech
- respect
- know-how
- trust
- flexibility
- tolerance for ambiguity
- sympathy
- patience
- rock bottom prices

Brazil

- extreme friendliness
- compassion
- mention Brazil
- cheerfulness
- mention football
- informality
- optimism
- relationship before product
- theatricality

Spain

- warmth
- originality
- eloquence
- liveliness
- strong eye contact
- humour
- overt body language
- charisma
- good price

Italy

- friendliness
- flexibility
- style
- tasteful product
- elegance
- well-dressed
- personality
- laughter
- some cultural reference
- delicacy
- design-conscious

Norway

- egalitarian approach
- brisk style
- quiet confidence in product
- no overstating
- clean design
- quality product
- technical information
- solidity

Russia

- official view is a lie
- personal view is true
- changes are always bad
- suspicious of foreigners
- expects rhetoric
- expects sentiment
- expects complexity
- needs recognition
- people-oriented
- conspiratorial
- no war talk
- dislikes greed

Netherlands

- recognition of Dutch inter-nationalism and incredible economic achievements
- interesting product
- facts, facts, facts
- no sarcasm, only few jokes
- lots of print
- no extravagance
- no time-wasting
- open discussion
- no hard sell
- show way to mutual profit
- well-prepared, well-informed speaker
- competence

Canada

- low key presentation
- technical facts
- no ostentation
- no hard sell
- plenty of context
- tolerance
- humour
- quick feedback and debate
- cultural sensitivity

Poland

- recognition
- logic
- sentiment
- distrust officials
- personal touch
- no pressure or brute force
- concessions
- favourable deal

Hungary

- theatricality
- verbosity
- humour
- feelings
- charm
- context
- respect
- artistry
- sophistication
- good deal

Africa

- warmth
- friendliness
- humanity
- sincerity
- trust
- no patronising
- ho hurry
- some humour
- no "jungle" words
- professional appearance
- concessions
- physical proximity

Leadership styles

Different cultures have diverse concepts of leadership. Leaders can be born, elected, or trained and groomed. Others seize power or have leadership thrust upon them. Leadership can be autocratic or democratic, collective or individual, meritocratic or unearned, desired or imposed.

It is not surprising that business leaders (managers) often wield their power in conformity with the national set-up – for instance a confirmed democracy like Sweden produces low key democratic managers; Arab managers are good Muslims; Chinese managers usually have government or Party affiliations.

Leaders cannot readily be transferred from culture to culture. Japanese Prime Ministers would be largely ineffective in the United States; American politicians would fare badly in most Arab countries; mullahs would not be tolerated in Norway. Similarly, business managers find the transition from one culture to another fraught with difficulties. Such transfers become more and more common with the globalisation of business, but the composition of international teams and particularly the choice of their leaders, requires careful thought. Autocratic French managers have to tread warily in consensus-minded Japan or Sweden. Courteous Asian leaders would have to adopt a more vigorous style in argumentative Holland or theatrical Spain if they wished to hold the stage. German managers sent to Australia are somewhat alarmed at the irreverence of their staff and their apparent lack of respect for authority.

Hispanic America

Leadership in most Hispanic American countries has traditionally been centred around a strong dictator or military figure or, in the case of Mexico and Argentina, dominant political parties. Nepotism is common and staff are manipulated by a variety of persuasive methods ranging from (benign) paternalism to outright exploitation and coercion.

Brazil

Leaders in Brazil have often been military officers or civilian strong men ruling with the approval of the army. The huge size of the economy has in recent years generated a large professional class which regulates the conduct of business on a day-to-day basis. The volatility of the economy often necessitates state interference.

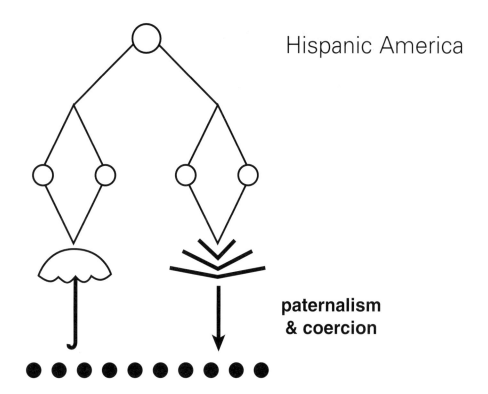

Hispanic America

paternalism & coercion

Brazil

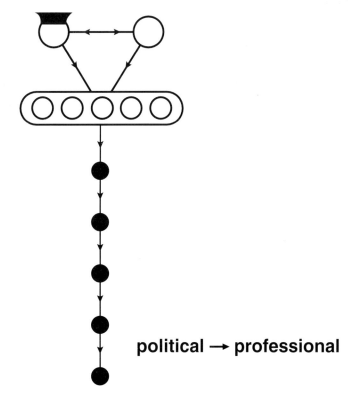

political → professional

Sweden

Swedish managers are the least autocratic in the world and sit in the ring consulting with all at executive level and often with quite subordinate staff members. It is said Swedish managers wield power by appearing non-powerful. This style, ubiquitous in Sweden and popular with Swedes, is hardly conducive to rapid decision-making.

UK

The class system persists to some extent in the UK and in some companies managers, though not entirely autocratic, maintain considerable power distance between themselves and their staff. More common today, however, is the rather casual manager who sits just outside the ring of executives, but is in close contact with them and well able to conduct effective supervision without interfering unduly with their daily routine.

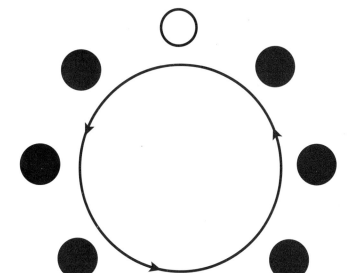

Sweden

primus inter pares

UK

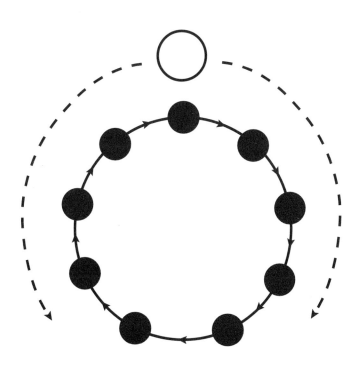

casual leadership

France

In France, authority is centred around the chief executive. Top managers, who have usually been groomed in one of the *grandes écoles*, are well-trained, charismatic and extremely autocratic. They often appear to consult with middle managers, technical staff – even workers, but decisions are generally personal and orders are topdown. Managers at this élite level are rarely fired when they make blunders.

Germany

The basic principle of German management is that you put the most experienced, best-educated person at the top and he/she instructs and guides meticulously his/her immediate inferior. Orders are passed down through the management structure in this manner. Though leadership is consequently hierarchical and autocratic, German leaders do listen to suggestions "from the factory floor", as German workers are generally well-educated and inventive. In this way, consensus plays a part in German business.

France

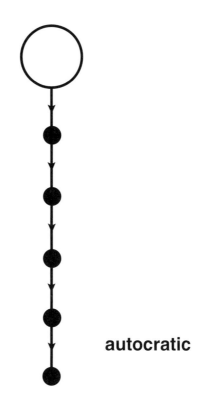

autocratic

Germany

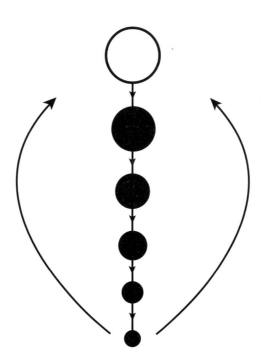

hierarchy + consensus

Finland

Finnish leaders, like many British, exercise control from a position just outside and above the ring of middle managers, who are allowed to make day-to-day decisions. Finnish top executives have the reputation of being decisive at crunch time and do not hesitate to stand shoulder to shoulder with staff and help out in crises.

Norway

In democratic Norway the boss is very much in the centre of things and staff enjoy access to him/her at most times. Middle managers' opinions are heard and acted upon in egalitarian fashion, but top executives rarely abandon responsibility and accountability.

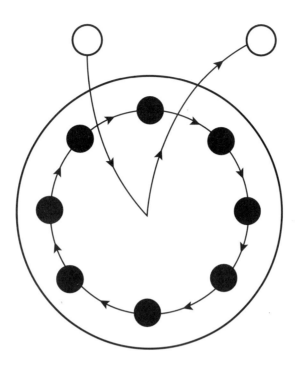

officer helps out in crisis

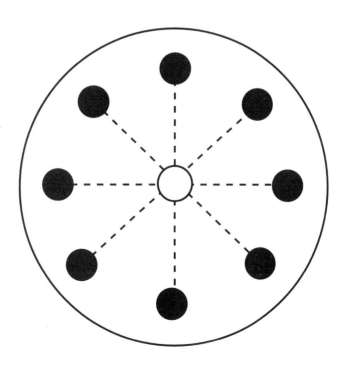

boss, but friendly

Denmark

Danish top executives and middle managers are not always clearly distinguishable to non-Danes. Managers of all levels mingle for decision-making and democratic procedures are mandatory. Though top managers can exert considerable pressure, Danes are skilful in maintaining a decidedly congenial atmosphere in discussion. Horizontal communication is widespread and generally successful.

USA

American leadership symbolises the vitality and audacity of the land of free enterprise. Management structure is pyramidical, with seniors driving and inspiring people under them. Americans are allowed to make individual decisions, but usually within the framework of corporate restrictions. Managers are capable of teamwork and corporate spirit, but value individual freedom more than company welfare. They are very mobile. They get fired if they make mistakes.

Denmark

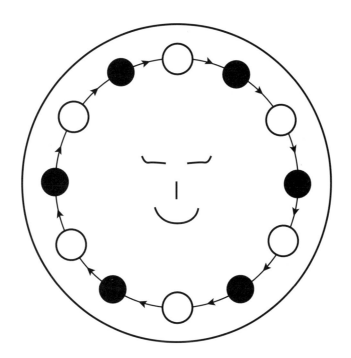

cosy, *(hygge)* all round

USA

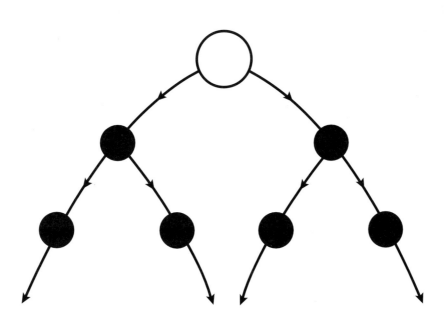

**structured individualism
speed, drive**

Canada

Canadian leaders are low key (compared with Americans), but often possess North American dynamism and are action-oriented. They normally sit in the ring of executives, with whom they confer democratically. A combination of professional competence and personal modesty makes them good leaders and, in international teams, good chairmen.

Australia

Australian managers, like Swedes, must sit in the ring with the "mates". From this position, once it is accepted that they will not pull rank, they actually exert much more influence than their Swedish counterparts, as the semi-Americanized nature of Australian business requires quick thinking and rapid decision-making.

Canada

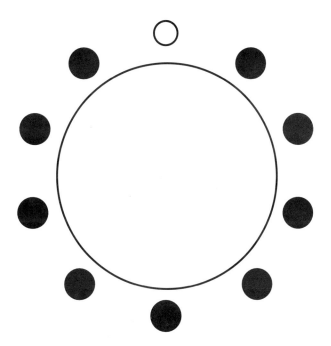

low key dynamo

Australia

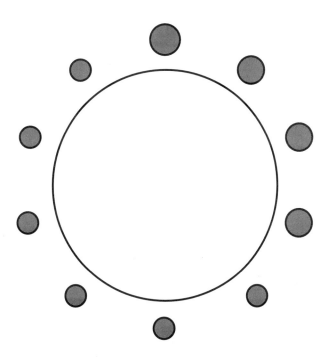

one of the mates

Netherlands

Leadership in the Netherlands is based on merit, competence and achievement. Managers are vigorous and decisive, but consensus is mandatory, as there are many key players in the decision-making process. Long "Dutch debates" lead to action, taken at the top, but with constant reference to the "ranks". Ideas from low levels are allowed to filter freely upwards in the hierarchy.

Indonesia

In colonial times, leadership came from the Dutch. Under Sukarno and Suharto leadership was exercised principally by the military and therefore autocratic. The indifferent nature of many Indonesians to the business process, has, however, resulted in a lot of business management being entrusted to a resident Chinese professional class, which has the commercial know-how and international connections. Overseas Chinese shareholding in many Indonesian companies encourages this situation.

Netherlands

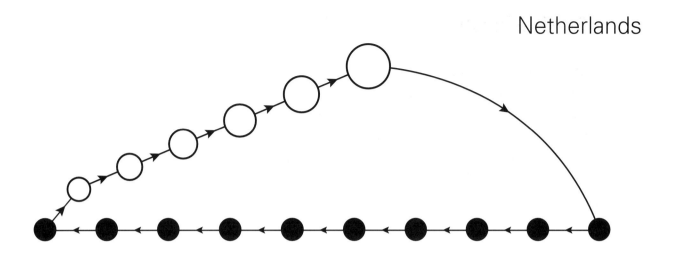

meritocratic, debating

Indonesia

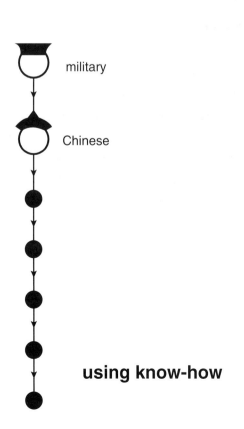

military

Chinese

using know-how

Arab countries

Arab leaders are often sheikhs and people connected with royal families.
There is consequently a lot of nepotism in Arab companies where sons,
nephews and brothers hold key positions. This applies particularly in the
Gulf States. In other Arab countries dictators influence business
leadership – often the military is involved.

India

Nepotism is also rife in traditional Indian companies. Family members
hold key positions and work in close unison. Policy is also dictated by
the trade group, e.g. fruit merchants, jewellers, etc. These groups work
in concert, often develop close personal relations (through intermarriage
etc.) and come to each other's support in difficult times.

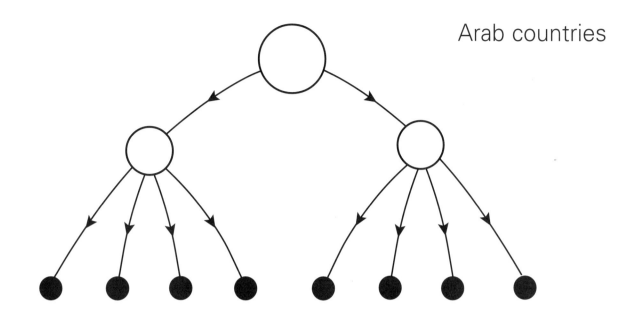

Arab countries

nepotism

India

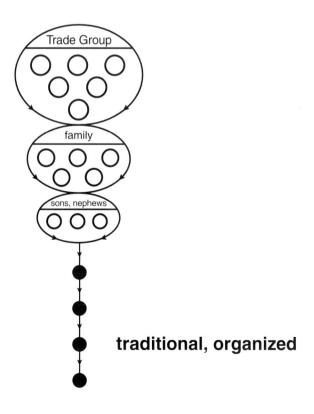

traditional, organized

Spain

Spanish leaders, like French, are autocratic and charismatic. Unlike the French, they work less from logic than intuition and pride themselves on their personal influence on all their staff members. Possessed often of great human force, they are able to persuade and inspire at all levels. Nepotism is also common in many companies. Declamatory in style, Spanish managers often see their decisions as irreversible.

Italy

Italian leadership is basically autocratic, but shows more flexibility than Spanish, as managers mingle easily with staff and intersperse themselves at many levels. There are many "clan" and group interests in the southern half of the country and loyalty to the leader is automatic and mandatory. In Milan, Turin and Genova, there is a growing tendency to select managers on merit. In the north in general professional competence is valued, though connections remain important.

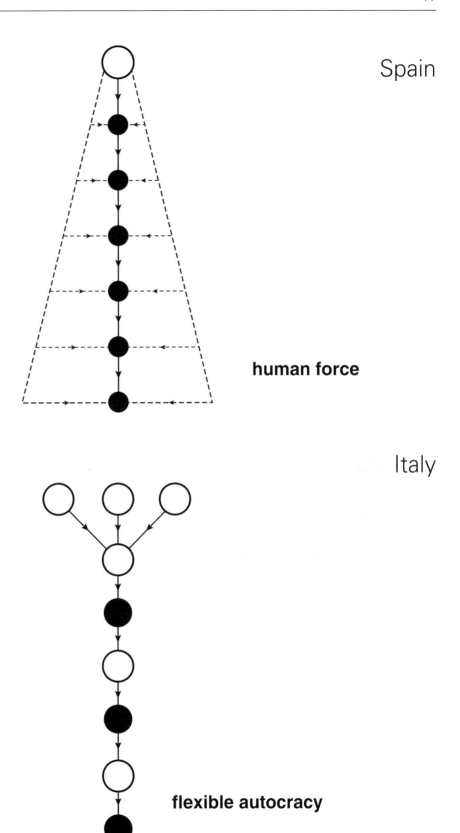

Spain

human force

Italy

flexible autocracy

China

Consensus is generally highly valued in China, but in companies controlled by the state a leadership group (often invisible) will decide policy. In the developing expansion of capitalist-style companies, leaders are emerging with reputations of competence, also locally-elected officials (e.g. mayors) are becoming influential in the business sphere and may have only loose ties with Beijing. In Chinese family businesses (and there are many) the senior male is the patriarch and the usual nepotic structure is observable.

Korea

Chaebols (conglomerates) control a lot of business in Korea. These were, and are, family-owned and nepotism is rampant with all sons, brothers, nephews etc. holding key positions. The very size of these conglomerates has, however, necessitated the introduction of a class of professional managers. These are now ubiquitous and growing in importance. Decision-making is therefore largely hybrid.

China

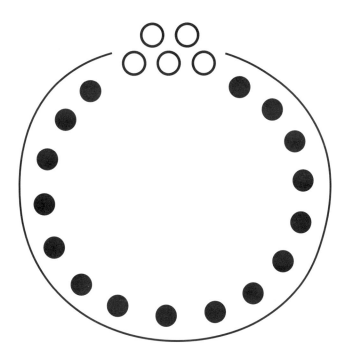

consensus with leadership group

Korea

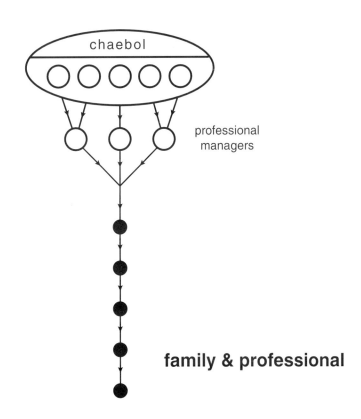

chaebol

professional
managers

family & professional

Japan

Japanese top executives have great power in conformity with Confucian hierarchy, but actually have little involvement in the everyday affairs of the company. On appropriate occasions they initiate policies which are conveyed to middle managers and rank and file. Ideas often originate on the factory floor or with other lower level sources. Signatures are collected among workers and middle managers as suggestions, ideas and inventions make their way up the company hierarchy. Many people are involved. Top executives take the final step in ratifying items which have won sufficient approval.

Russia

The leadership concept is undergoing profound changes in Russia following the demise of the Soviet Communist state. Efforts made by managers to promote business through official channels only are likely to founder on the rocks of bureaucracy and Russian apathy. Using key people and personal alliances, the "system" is often by-passed and a result achieved.

Japan

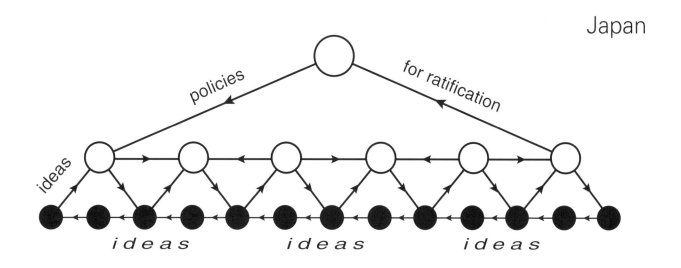

ideas   ideas   ideas

ringi-sho consensus

Russia

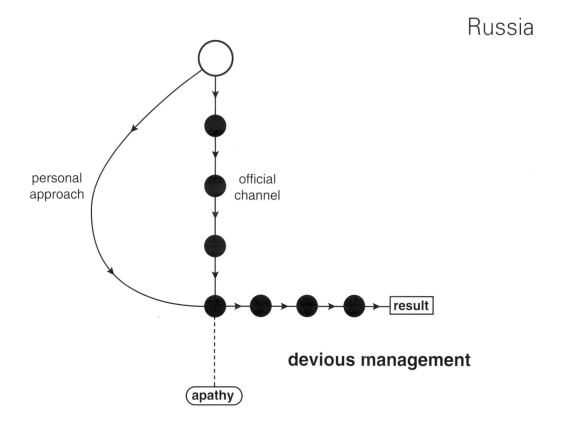

devious management

Language of management

Among the tasks of managers are the necessities of instructing, motivating and leading their subordinates. They may often lead by example, but as far as motivation and the issuance of directives are concerned, they will be heavily dependent on language. Different languages are used in different ways and with a variety of effects. Hyperbolic American and understated British English clearly inform and inspire listening staff with separate allure and driving force. Managers of all nationalities know how to speak to their compatriots to best effect, for there are built-in characteristics in their language which facilitate the conveyance of ideas to their own kind. They are in fact only vaguely aware of their dependence on these linguistic traits which make their job easier. With increasing globalisation, problems will arise in the following instances:

(a) when managers are involved in international team building.

(b) when they have to use a language other than their own.

An example of situation (a) is when a Briton or American addresses a team containing, among others, Germans. The occasional quipping or half-serious remarks typical of Anglo-American managers will only too often be taken literally by Germans, who may carry out "orders" which were only being casually considered.

An example of (b) is when a Japanese managing Anglo-Saxons hints at directives in such a courteous and half-suggestive manner that all is lost in a fog of impeccable politeness. How does the particular genius of a certain language, manifested by its structure, vocabulary and tones, play its part in conveying instructions and inspiration to its listeners? Let us examine some of the characteristics of languages which are tools of management in parts of the industrialized world.

Australia

Australian English is young, vibrant, inventive, humorous, cynical, irreverent, classless, human, original, often teetering between erudite and vulgar – in short a revealing reflection of the "battling" Australian character. As such it is the key to how Australians may be motivated. Australian managers would be ineffective with American pep talk English. (Australians would respond cynically). British or Canadian English, on the other hand, would be too prim or too laid back. The Aussies want their boss to join them in a healthy respect for rules and formalism, to lapse into broad speech and cuss a bit, to be affable and ironic at the same time, to avoid flowery or obscure expressions – finally, to call a spade a spade.

France

French managers inhabit quite a different world. They are clinically direct in their approach and see no advantage in ambiguity or ambivalence. The French language is a crisp, incisive tongue, a kind of verbal dance or gymnastics of the mouth, which presses home its points with an undisguised, logical urgency. It is rational, precise, ruthless in its clarity.

The French education system, from childhood, places a premium on articulateness and eloquence of expression. Unlike Japanese, Finnish or British children, French children are rarely discouraged from being talkative. In the French culture loquacity is equated with intelligence and silence does not have a particularly golden sheen. *Lycée*, university and *École normale supérieure* education reinforces the emphasis on good speaking, purity of grammar and mastery of the French idiom. The French language, unquestionably, is the chief weapon wielded by managers in directing, motivating and dominating their staff. Less articulate French people will show no resentment. Masterful use of language and logic implies, in their understanding, masterful management.

Australia

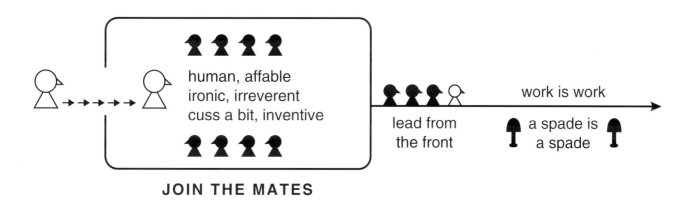

human, affable
ironic, irreverent
cuss a bit, inventive

JOIN THE MATES

lead from
the front

work is work

a spade is
a spade

France

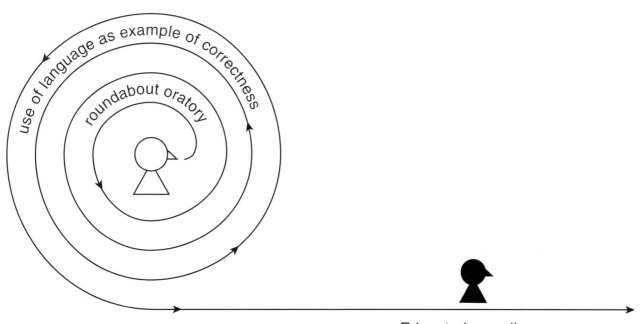

use of language as example of correctness

roundabout oratory

Educated compliance

USA

In the USA the manager, if not always a hero, is viewed in a positive and sympathetic light, as one of the figures responsible for the nation's speedy development and commercial services. The US is a young, vigorous, ebullient nation and its language reflects the national energy and enthusiasm. Americans exaggerate in order to simplify – low-key Britons feel they go 'over the top', but the dynamic cliché wears well in the United States.

The frequent tendency to hyperbolise, exaggerating chances of success, overstating aims or targets etc., allows American managers to 'pump up' their subordinates – to drive them on to longer hours and speedier results. American salespeople do not resist this approach, for they are used to the 'hard sell' themselves. Tough talk, quips, wisecracks, barbed repartee – all available in good supply in American English – help them on their way.

The ubiquitous use of 'get' facilitates clear, direct orders. You get up early, you get going, you get there first, you get the client and you get the order, got it? The many neologisms in American English, used liberally by managers, permit them to appear up-to-date, aphoristic, humorous and democratic.

UK

In Britain the language has quite different qualities and, as a management tool, is much more subtle. British staff members who would be put off by American exaggeration and tough talk fall for a more understated, laid-back version of English which reflects their own characteristics. Managers manipulate subordinates with friendly small talk, humour, reserved statements of objectives and a very casual approach to getting down to work. You don't arrive on the dot and work round the clock. The variety of types of humour available in the UK enables managers to be humorous, to praise, change direction, chide, insinuate and criticise at will. They may even level criticism at themselves. Irony is a powerful weapon either way.

USA

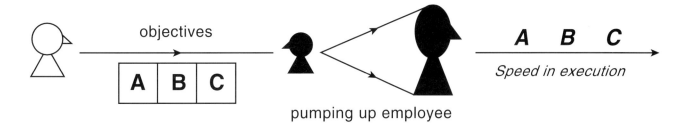

objectives

A B C

pumping up employee

A B C

Speed in execution

UK

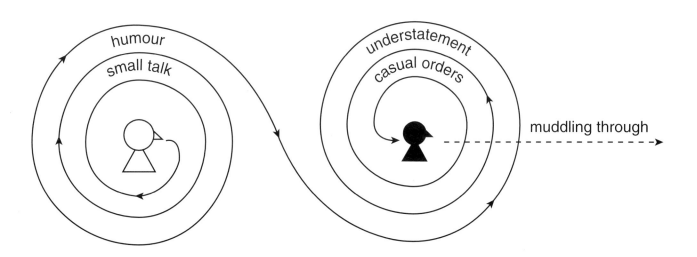

humour

small talk

understatement

casual orders

muddling through

Japan

There is a certain similarity in the language of management in Britain and Japan, although the basic and ever-present indirectness of the Japanese style makes the British, by comparison, seem clinical thinkers! In Japan the drive towards harmony is so strong that it takes priority over clarity, even over truth.

Japanese managers do not issue orders: they only hint at what has to be done. The language is custom designed for this. The structure, which normally stacks up a line of subordinate clauses before the main one, invariably lists the justifications for the directive before it reaches the listener. 'Complete September's final report by 5:30 pm' comes out in Japanese as: "It's 10th October today, isn't it? Our controller hasn't asked to see September's report yet. I wonder if he'll pop round tomorrow. You never know with him…" The actual order is never given – there is no need, the staff are already scrambling to their books.

Japanese has built-in mechanisms creating a strong impact on the listener. The general mandatory politeness creates a climate where staff appear to be quietly consulted in the most courteous manner. This very courtesy encourages their support and compliance. In fact they have no choice, as the hierarchy of communication is already settled by the status of the manager based on the quality and date of his university degree. The use of honorifics, moreover, reinforces the hierarchical situation. The different set of expressions (again mandatory) used in formulating the subordinates' responses to the manager's remarks closes the circle of suggestion, absorption, compliance.

Other features of the Japanese language which serve managers in instructing and motivating staff are the passive voice, used for extra politeness; the impersonal verb, which avoids casting direct blame; and the use of silence on certain issues, which indicates clearly to the subordinate what the manager's opinion is.

Korea

Compared to Japanese (to which it is related) the Korean language is less vague and is wielded more forcefully in a somewhat guttural manner. This suits the authoritarian directness of tough Korean managers who beat about the bush much less than Japanese or Chinese. *Kibun*, however, must be protected.

Japan

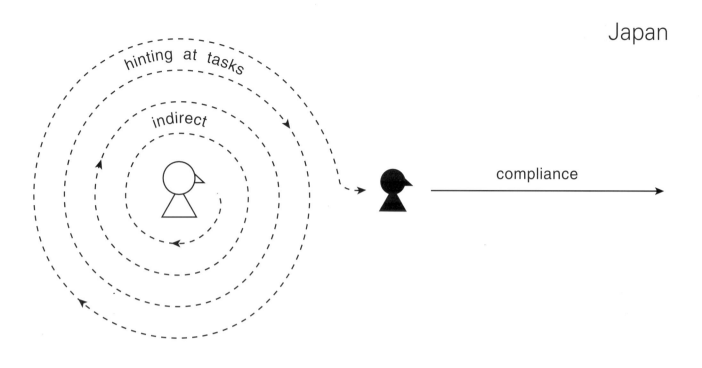

Korea

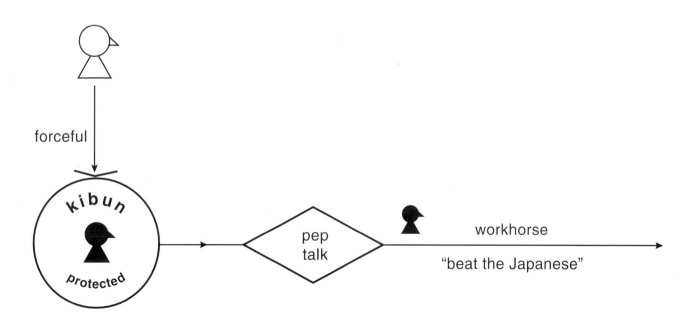

Sweden

Swedish is the democratic language par excellence. As a language of management it leans heavily on the *Du* form and dry, courteous expressions which clearly stratify managers at the same level as their colleagues or, at the very worst, as *primi inter pares*. I recently heard a TV journalist in his mid-twenties address the prime minister as *Du*.

Spain

To take a very different example, Spanish is directed towards staff at a much more vertical angle. Spanish managers are usually happy to use the *tu* form to subordinates, but the declaimed nature of their delivery, with typical Spanish fire and emphasis, makes their pronouncements and opinions virtually irreversible. Spanish, with its wealth of dimunitive endings, its rich vocabulary and multiple choice options on most nouns, is extremely suitable for expressing emotion, endearments, nuances and intimacies. Spanish managers' discourse leans on emotive content. They woo, persuade, cajole. They want you to know how they feel. The language exudes warmth, excitement, sensuousness, ardour, ecstasy and sympathy.

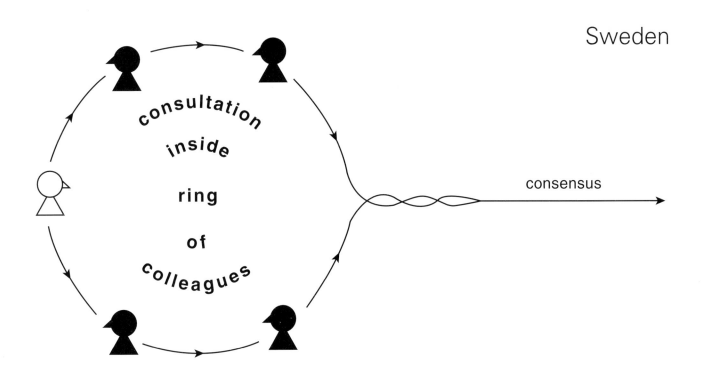

Sweden

consultation
inside
ring
of
colleagues

consensus

Spain

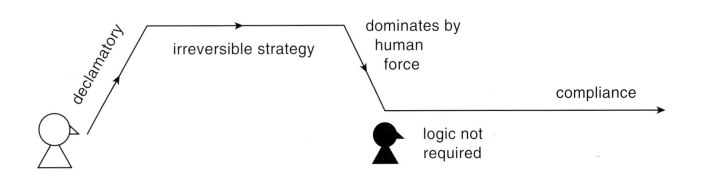

declamatory

irreversible strategy

dominates by
human
force

compliance

logic not
required

Norway

Norwegian managers addressing their staff have a strong and effective linguistic tool at their disposal. Spoken Norwegian is brisk, strident and cheerful – it has a fresh-air style about it. The distinctive, emphatic, rising tones of the language emphasize the Norway-centredness of the medium, serving to link managers more closely to their staff. It is not too low key and hints at great energy. Essentially democratic, the recent standardisation of the language (since the 1950s) enables the manager to identify with all Norwegians and to confirm he/she is "with it".

Denmark

Danish is a less strident language than Norwegian, less deliberate than Swedish. It excels in confiding, almost conspiratorial tones, enabling the manager to share ideas in a closely confidential manner with colleagues, among whom he/she mingles. Danish is low key, calm, serious but with hidden shafts of humour. It bespeaks long experience and wisdom. The Kingdom of Denmark has been around for over 1000 years. Controlled organisation and "small-and-quiet is beautiful" is the essence of the tongue.

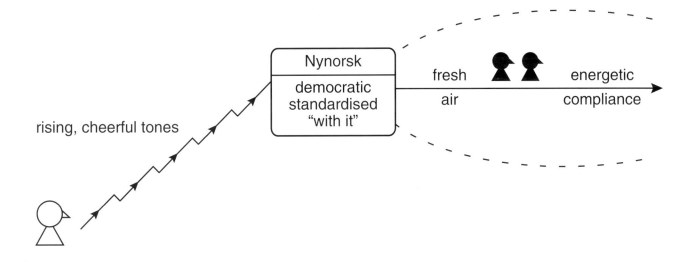

Norway

rising, cheerful tones

Nynorsk

democratic
standardised
"with it"

fresh
air

energetic
compliance

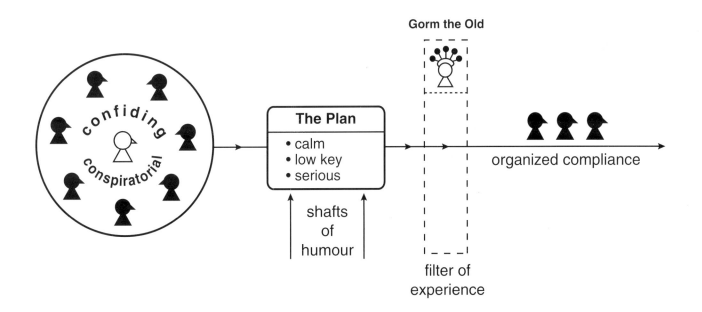

Denmark

confiding
conspiratorial

The Plan

• calm
• low key
• serious

shafts
of
humour

Gorm the Old

filter of
experience

organized compliance

Finland

Finnish management, though basically democratic, differs slightly from that of its Scandinavian neighbours inasmuch as the decisive, strong man type plays a greater role when things get bogged down. Finnish bosses are not averse to blowing hot and cold when they want things from their staff. They can be cold, terse and factual in one mode, then switch to a richer, more flowery one when it suits their purpose. Finnish – an eastern tongue – is more vibrant and sinewy than Scandinavian languages, with a much richer, adjective-strewn vocabulary, an army of manipulative particles and no fewer than 14 case-endings. These features give the speaker far more linguistic options than one can call on in most languages. Finnish managers are generally well educated, keep richness of expression in reserve in general day-to-day address, but occasionally "pull out all the stops" when praise, encouragement or reprimand are appropriate.

Italy

Which adjectives best describe the Italian language, known the world over for its pleasing effect on the ear? Soft, fluent, melodious, elegant, aesthetic, musical, pliant, seductive are some that come to mind. These terms indeed reflect the style of Italian managers as they seek to instruct, influence, persuade and perhaps charm their staff to comply with their requirements. Italians are cultured, finicky listeners who would be alienated by authoritarian German, exaggerated, simplified American, cacophonous gobbled Dutch or glottal Danish. They expect to be addressed with elegance and refinement, to be subtly manipulated, perhaps skilfully cajoled, but always in a medium corresponding to their civilised state, sense of aesthetics and acute awareness. The Italian language, spoken by an educated native, can satisfy all these needs.

Finland

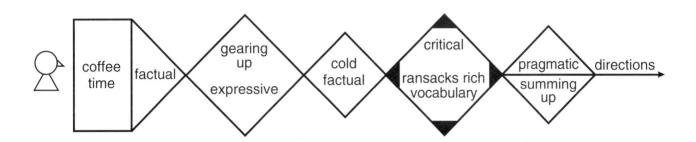

Italy

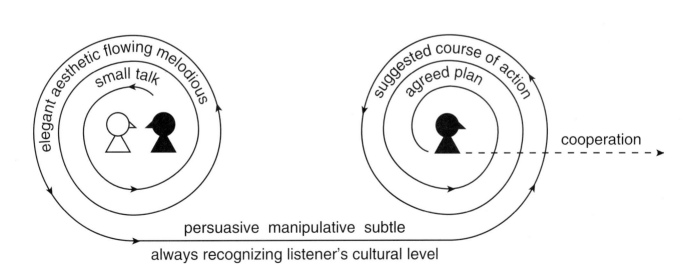

Hispanic America

The varieties of Spanish spoken in Latin America, from Mexico to Tierra del Fuego, differ considerably in accent and vocabulary according to the region, but they all have a common thread which distinguishes them clearly from Castilian Spanish – they are softer and gentler than the tongue of Castile, using a greater number of diminutives and avoiding the forceful "j" and "ll" sounds of central Spain as well as the ubiquitous lisp (c) of the Spanish court. The language of management of Castilian bosses is declamatory, strident, often harsh, usually irreversible. That of their Latin American counterparts tends to soften the delivery and the message, conveying in the gentleness of the language forms the compassionate style of an Amerindian-influenced continent which understands and accompanies human problems and suffering. Declamation and rhetoric are still present, but a subtle search for agreement and approval can be detected in a certain muting of tone and sound.

Brazil

There is a parallel difference between Brazilian and European Portuguese on the one hand and Latin American Spanish and Castilian on the other. Brazilians, like Latin Americans, avoid the harsher sounds of European Portuguese, employ more diminutives and forms of endearment and generally use the language with more exuberance and abandon than their Iberian cousins.

The language as such is an admirable tool for the Brazilian manager addressing staff, who are very concerned with cosiness and cheerfulness, freedom of expression and extroversion, sometimes racial harmony. Brazilian Portuguese revels in democratic forms, facility of delivery and avoidance of stiffness and formality.

Hispanic America

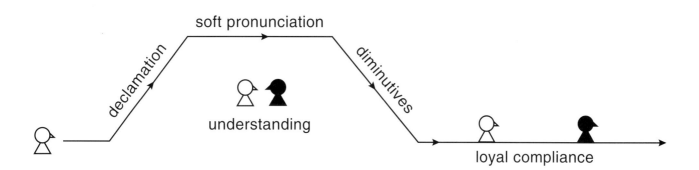

Brazil

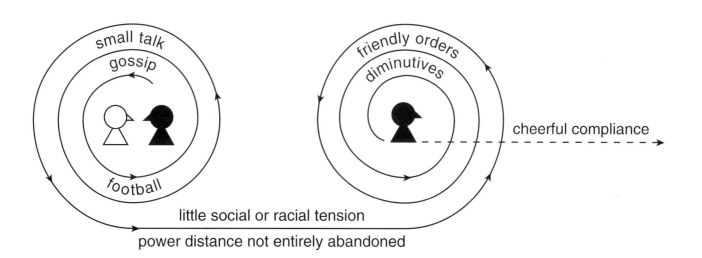

Netherlands

Gobble-gobble Dutch, sister language to German, has a similar
disciplined structure but is more folksy and less authoritarian than the
latter. The tight grammar, allied to an absence of pretence to elegance,
suits the tough, but give-and-take style of the Dutch manager.

Indonesia

The Indonesian national language – bahasa – is an artificial construct,
being an adaptation of nearby Malay. As there are hundreds of different
dialects spoken throughout the Indonesian islands, the government
needed a national medium to achieve some kind of linguistic unity. All
Indonesians therefore speak at least two languages.

     Bahasa has many of the characteristics of its Polynesian
cousins. It is essentially a respect language which avoids giving offence
to others and has constructions which protect face: oblique forms of
criticism, ritualistic utterances, etc. Indonesian managers motivate staff
with such softnesses. Because of the military influence, there are also,
however, nuances stressing the necessity for unity and occasionally
implications of coercion. Chinese managers, who conduct a lot of
business, speak bahasa fluently. Many of them were born in Indonesia.

Netherlands

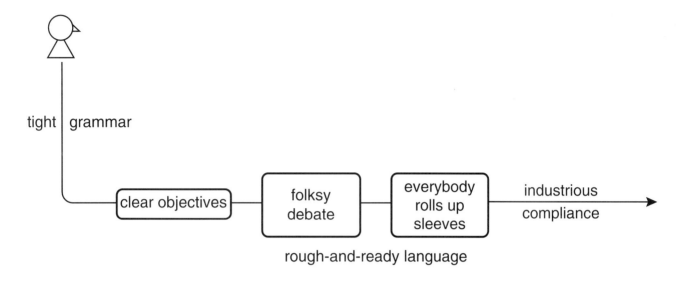

tight | grammar

clear objectives — folksy debate — everybody rolls up sleeves → industrious compliance

rough-and-ready language

Indonesia

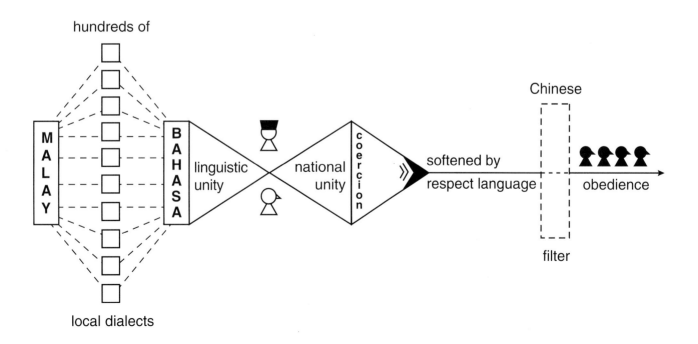

hundreds of

MALAY

BAHASA

linguistic unity

national unity

coercion

softened by respect language

Chinese

filter

obedience

local dialects

China

There are many varieties of Chinese, though Mandarin is in gradual ascendancy. Cantonese, and Shanghainese are, however, likely to retain their importance as languages of commerce.

Mandarin sounds authoritative to many Chinese and commands obedience. Chinese managers rely heavily on Confucian precepts, which support their authority to no small degree. Their language implies the 5 unequal relationships as taken for granted; it is delivered softly, implying Confucian standards of wisdom, kindness, moderation and frugality. Like most Asian tongues, it thrives on a certain ambiguity. Politeness and courtesy are mandatory. Subordinates are invariably wooed by this linguistic style.

India

The language of management in India is spoken in many tongues, though at higher levels it is often English. The characteristics of Indian English reflect Indian psychology, so that when Hindi, Urdu, Bengali etc. are used, there will be many commonalities in the approach.

Indian English is old-fashioned, flowery and verbose. It is essentially a human, sympathetic language showing respect and often humility to the listener. It is generous in praise, yet reluctant to criticise, since failure in Indian business may quickly be attributed to bad karma. Indian English excels in ambiguity and such things as truth and appearances are often subject to negotiation. Above all, the language of the Indian manager emphasizes the collective nature of the task and challenge. India is far from being a classless society, but the groups will often stand or fall together in the hard world of the sub-continent.

China

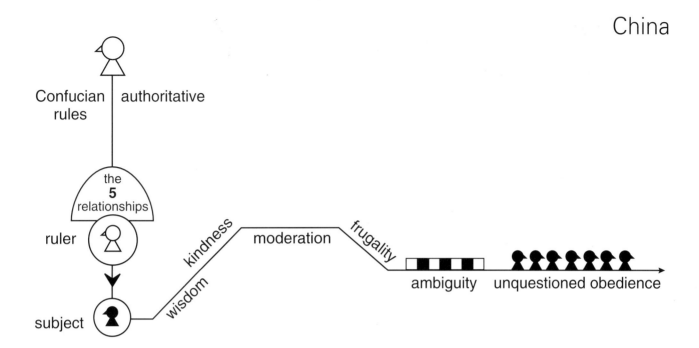

India

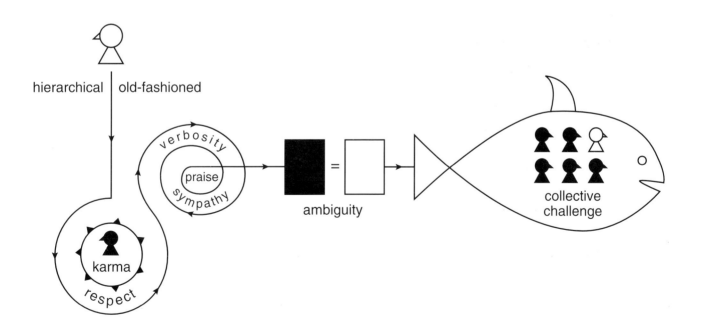

Canada

Canadian speech is Americanized British English or muted Anglicized American, depending on which way you look at it. It is low key, humorous and pleasing and is an excellent tool for motivating laid-back, calm, modest, tolerant staff. Canadian managers will avoid the vague stuffiness of some of their English counterparts, but they will be even more careful to shun American pushiness, hard sell or over-simplification.

Russia

Nigel Holden sees Russian, where social distance is encoded in highly subtle ways, as resembling Japanese as a flexible management language in network mode. Soviet managers were involved little in such areas as leadership or motivation of employees. The management style utilised threats and coercion to produce results demanded by socialist 'planning'. How Russian will develop as a language of management in the future will depend on modes of address using names and titles and the development of formal and informal mechanisms which do not remind subordinates of coercion and control.

Canada

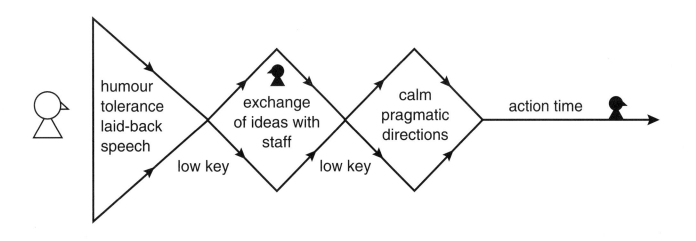

Russia

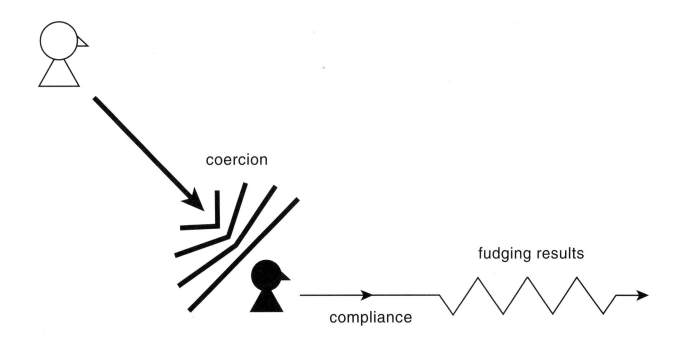

Germany

Germans belong to a data-oriented, low context culture and like receiving detailed information and instruction to guide them in the performance of tasks at which they wish to excel. In business situations German is not used in a humorous way, neither do its rigid case-endings and strict word order allow the speaker to think aloud very easily. With few homonyms (in contrast, for example, to Chinese) and a transparent word-building system, the language is especially conducive to the issuing of clear orders. The almost invariable use of the *Sie* form in business fits in well with the expectation of obedience and reinforces the hierarchical nature of the communication.

As far as motivating subordinates is concerned, German would seem to be less flexible than, for instance, bubbly American English. The constrictive effect of case-endings makes it difficult for German speakers to chop and change in the middle of a sentence. They embark on a course, plotted partly by gender, partly by morphology, in a straitjacket of Teutonic word order. The verb coming at the end obliges the hearer to listen carefully in order to extract the full meaning. The length and complexity of German sentences reflect the German tendency to distrust simple utterances. Information-hungry Germans are among the best listeners in the world; their language fits the bill.

Arab countries

In the Gulf States a good manager is a good Moslem. The language used will make frequent references to Allah and align itself with the precepts and style of the Koran. A didactic management style is the result. The inherent rhetorical qualities of the Arabic language lend themselves to reinforcing the speaker's sincerity. A raised voice is a sign not of anger, but of genuine feeling and exhortation.

Germany

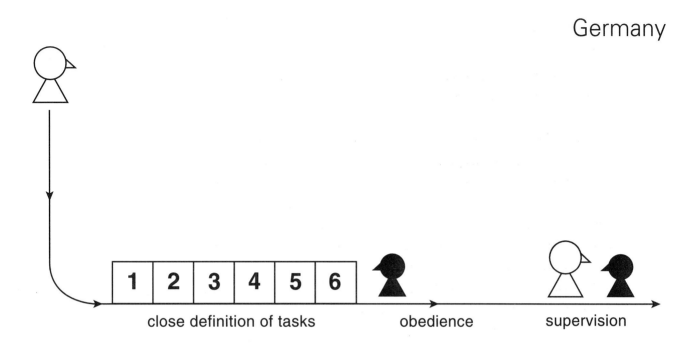

close definition of tasks obedience supervision

Arab countries

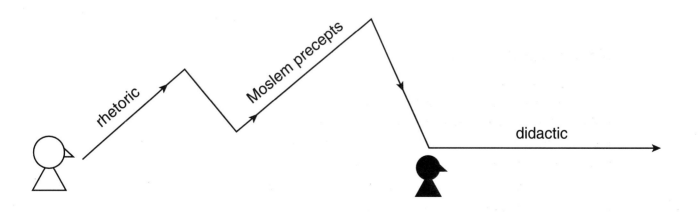

rhetoric

Moslem precepts

didactic

About Richard D. Lewis

Richard D. Lewis has been active in the fields of applied and anthropological linguistics for over 35 years. His work in several fields of communicative studies has involved him in the organisation of courses and seminars for many of the world's leading industrial and financial companies.

In 1961 he pioneered the world's first English by Television series, produced by Suomen Televisio and subsequently was script writer for the first BBC series, "Walter and Connie", in 1962.

He has lived and worked in several European countries, where his clients included ABB, Allianz, Banco de España, Banque de France, Deutsche Bank, Ericsson, Fiat, Gillette, IBM, Mercedes Benz, Nestlé, Nokia, Saab and Volvo.

He also spent 5 years in Japan where he was tutor to Empress Michiko and other members of the Japanese Imperial Family. During this period, his services were requested by firms such as Nomura, Mitsubishi, Hitachi, Sanyo, Mitsui and Nippon Steel.

More recently he has been heavily involved in the intercultural field, founding companies in France, Germany, Spain, Italy and Brazil, teaching communication skills in these countries as well as Finland, Sweden, the United Kingdom and the USA.

Mr Lewis, who speaks 10 European and 2 Asiatic languages, is currently chairman of Richard Lewis Communications plc, an international institute of language and cross-cultural training with offices in over a dozen countries. His recent book *When Cultures Collide* is regarded as the classic work on intercultural issues and was the Spring main selection of the US Book of the Month Club in 1997.

Mr Lewis was knighted by President Ahtisaari of Finland in March 1997.

When Cultures Collide

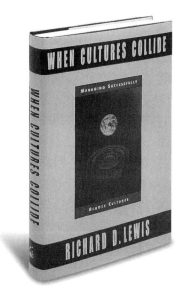

In *When Cultures Collide*, Richard Lewis provides a truly global and practical guide to working and communicating across cultures, explaining how our own culture and language affect the ways in which we organise our world, think, feel and respond, before going on to suggest both general and specific ways of making our influence felt across the cultural divide.

There are penetrating insights into how different business cultures accord status, structure their organisations and view the role of leader, alongside invaluable advice on global negotiation, sales and marketing. The book ranges from differences in etiquette and body language to new thinking in the area of international management and team-building in Europe and the USA, as well as covering challenging new geographical ground in Russia, China and the Far East.

By focusing on the cultural roots of national behaviour, both in society and business, we can foresee and calculate with a surprising degree of accuracy how others will react and respond to us. Lewis adds the often overlooked dimension of language – for example, how Japanese often react in a certain way because they are thinking in Japanese.

When Cultures Collide gives you a greater understanding of what makes other people tick and enables managers to ensure that their policies and activities exploit cultural synergies and make the right appeal to their chosen market.

When Cultures Collide is published by Nicholas Brealey Publishing and is available from Richard Lewis Communications. Please call on +44 1962 771111, fax on +44 1962 771355, or email info@crossculture.com. You may also order directly from our website: www.crossculture.com.